Investing for Kids

*Learn How Money Works and
Grow Your Financial Literacy*

Isaac A. Robertson

© **Copyright 2021 - All rights reserved.**

The content contained within this book may not be reproduced, duplicated or transmitted without direct written permission from the author or the publisher.

Under no circumstances will any blame or legal responsibility be held against the publisher, or author, for any damages, reparation, or monetary loss due to the information contained within this book, either directly or indirectly.

Legal Notice:

This book is copyright protected. It is only for personal use. You cannot amend, distribute, sell, use, quote or paraphrase any part, or the content within this book, without the consent of the author or publisher.

Disclaimer Notice:

Please note the information contained within this document is for educational and entertainment purposes only. All effort has been executed to present accurate, up to date, reliable, complete information. No warranties of any kind are declared or implied. Readers acknowledge that the author is not engaged in the rendering of legal, financial, medical or professional advice. The content within this book has been derived from various sources. Please consult a licensed professional before attempting any techniques outlined in this book.

By reading this document, the reader agrees that under no circumstances is the author responsible for any losses, direct or indirect, that are incurred as a result of the use of the information contained within this document, including, but not limited to, errors, omissions, or inaccuracies.

TABLE OF CONTENTS

Introduction 1
    Learning the Value of a Dollar 1
Chapter 1: What Should You Know About Money? 3
    Earning and Saving Your Money 5
        Heading to the Bank 11
Chapter 2: Are You Interested in Interest? 23
    Not-That-Simple Interest 24
        Let's Talk About Equity 27
        Real Estate 29
Chapter 3: The Good, the Bad, and the Ugly Investments .. 32
    Stocks and Bonds 35
        Cryptocurrency 39
        Meet Jaydyn Carr 40
Conclusion 42
    Saving is Super 42
References 44

Introduction

What have you learned about money so far? That it doesn't grow on trees? Well, that is true, but there is more to know about money and finances that can help you understand and do some smart saving for your future. You have probably been with your parents to buy groceries or shopping for clothes and toys. There is more to it than handing over a credit card and leaving the store with bags full of goodies. Follow all the tips and advice in this book, and you will have a good foot forward when it comes to earning, spending, and saving money.

Learning the Value of a Dollar

Why is it so important to understand money and saving? Making wise choices with your money will be good for you in the long run. Not to say that saving up for something you really want is not something you should do. It is important to understand that making money and working hard for it is something that will build you up and make you a better person. Working hard for what you want and achieving your goals of saving can make you feel happy and accomplished.

Do not buy something you know you cannot afford. If you are interested in something more expensive, it is smart to research it online and be patient with the decision. If weeks or months down the road you still really want it as bad as you did when you first saw it, you are probably ready to purchase it. You might even see that later on, that thing you want is on sale. It was $20 yesterday, but now it's only $10!

When you finally make that purchase after saving up your money for it, it feels so good knowing how hard you worked for it. Getting your allowance from chores or helping out during the spring when it's time to mow the lawn will start making your piggy bank burst with coins and dollar bills. Don't spend it all at once! Be smart with your money, and you will feel much better about buying things you want.

Chapter 1: What Should You Know About Money?

It seems like everything you need these days costs money. Money can also get you into trouble if you are not careful. It can be your enemy, and it can be your best friend. Just like your best friend, it depends on how you treat them. If you treat your best friend nicely, they will treat you the same. If you abuse your friend, they probably won't be sticking around. But what even is money anyways?

Money is what we use to pay for any goods, like a new toy. We also use it for services, like paying someone to paint your house. Currency is money that is in circulation where you live, such as coins and bills.

Don't be afraid to start early with understanding money, knowing what it looks like, and being able to count it properly. Learning how to count money and coins is important. It's also important to know how to make change, which is the way we decide how much money someone gets back when they give us too much. For example, if you buy something that is $15, and you give the cashier a $20 bill, you will receive $5 back in change. If something is $12.65, you can always count out your pennies, quarters, dimes, and nickels to make the exact amount, and no change will be owed to you. If you buy something with cash, you should be able to figure out in your head the amount that is owed back to you, just to be safe. Remember: Be smart and be careful with your money.

> Fun Fact! Thank goodness for the era when canned foods were out and wholesome natural and organic food was in. In the early 1970's, many stores started selling organic, fresh food rather than only food sold in a can.

When you are shopping, and something is on sale, it is helpful to be able to figure out in your head how much will be taken off your item. Then you will know for sure that you have enough money to purchase it. For example, if something is 40% off, this is a great opportunity to use some of your math knowledge. Knowing your percentages will come in handy when you want to figure out how much you will be saving when something is on sale, but it also comes in handy when you have to tip waiters and waitresses at restaurants.

Ask your parents/guardians about ways that you can help save money around the home. It can be as easy as turning off the water when you brush your teeth. You have to pay bills in order to have gas, electricity, and even water in your home, and if you use a lot of it when you only need to use some, you're throwing money away that you could be saving for something else. Help out around the house by turning the light out when you leave a room or taking efficient–short but still making sure you are clean–showers. It is also helping out our planet.

Fun Fact! Before cash and coins were used to pay for goods and services, money came in the form of cattle, animal hide, cacao beans, and even precious stones. We're talking back in 9,000 B.C. Whatever was looked at as important in society at the time could be used to pay for things.

Earning and Saving Your Money

When you finally start to earn your own money, you will feel more independent, especially if you have saved up your money for something you really want. If you earn some money by working hard, and you decide to hold onto it, the longer you keep earning and putting it away, the bigger it will grow, and you can have something you really want to save up for instead of a smaller, less exciting purchase by spending it. But how do I get money? What's a good way to save money? What if my dog keeps eating it? What if my little sister keeps stealing it and using it to buy candy and then pretending it didn't happen?

Well, first things first, get that dollar bill out of Fido's mouth, and keep your money in a hidden spot so your sister won't find it. This is your money, and you don't want others to take what you worked so hard to get.

Now that we have a gameplan to protect it, how do we get it in the first place? Earning money can be easy at home, and you can get creative with your talents and try to earn money in many ways. If you are crafty, why not turn some of your artistic flair into something you can sell? With the help of an adult, you can get the word out and tell your friends and neighbors. This way of getting the word out about products you have to sell is called marketing, and it's a great way to boost your popularity with people who want what you made.

Be aware of the changing seasons. There is always something needing to be done outside. In the winter, consider going around your neighborhood offering to shovel driveways for a small fee. In the summer, you can mow lawns, and in the fall, you can rake leaves. Find out about your local paper and see if you can get a route going for yourself. Make sure that you can get a parent or adult to accompany you if you plan to stray away from your home.

Fun Fact! China is the inventor of paper money. Not only do they produce a lot of the toys we buy today, in the 7th century, they decided carrying around all those copper coins was too heavy. Paper notes were introduced, and they quickly became a more popular option.

Talking about all that work made me exhausted! An ice cream cone on a hot day or a cup of cocoa in the winter is a great way to reward yourself for all that hard work. It is important to reward yourself when you do a good job of saving money. As much as we value being careful with our money and having self-control, we have to even it out a bit with some occasional fun and rewards.

When it comes to bigger purchases though, it is important to do research. With today's technologies, you can do research on anything from a new game to a new pair of sneakers. Check out the reviews online for products. With the help of a parent or guardian, look at multiple websites that are reliable and honest. Read reviews that customers like yourself left, and make sure what you're getting has good quality and doesn't have a lot of issues.

But what if nothing sounds good right now? What will I do with all this money? One good idea is to ask an adult about opening a savings account. Having money in your savings account is always smart, especially when you get older and are thinking about renting or owning your home. Keeping a stash of money in case of emergencies will be helpful because you never know what could happen in a day. It also collects overtime with something called interest, which we'll get to a little later. For now, know that it will help you get money just by putting it in the account.

We mentioned researching products to buy in stores, but we all know we don't have to jump in a car to buy things anymore. Online shopping is so much easier, but there are some important things we need to know before jumping onto eBay.

The world wide web can be a deceiving place, and it is way too easy to spend more than you planned online. With Amazon on the rise, you can look up just about anything and purchase it with a credit card or debit card. There are a lot of different scams lingering around online, so make sure that the website and seller you are buying from can be trusted. Again, do your research with the help of a parent or guardian, and make sure it is a trustworthy company.

Here are just a few tips and tricks to make sure that you and your money isn't being taken advantage of.
1. Make sure you always have a tracking number attached to anything you buy online. That way, you know where it is coming from and approximately how long until you will receive it.
2. Don't give out any of your personal information online. People can use this information to hack into accounts and steal items and money.
3. Always get a parent/guardian's permission before purchasing anything online. They can help you decide which deals are best, which companies are trustworthy, and if the product has good quality.

4. If someone that you've never met asks you to pay them with a gift card or a wireless transfer, think twice. This is most likely a scam.

5. Whenever you receive an email or even a text from an unknown source that looks like they want you to click on a link, don't do it. By clicking on it, the scammer can retrieve all of your personal info. It may look like a recognizable company or brand, but you can tell by the recipient's email if it is legitimate.

6. Resist the urge to click on something just because it tells you that you have a certain time frame before the deal is up. Red flag for a big scam!

7. Be careful with who you meet online, and always be cautious about the details you put on social media.

8. Buy local! It's better for your community, and it's much safer.

9. Use a safe payment method when purchasing online.

One of those safe payment methods we just talked about is PayPal. This is a wonderful way to pay for the items you want online. You don't have to enter your credit information for every purchase, so it makes it much safer. Any time you make a purchase, just choose the PayPal option, and you're done! You can also easily transfer funds from other PayPal users. Just be sure to create an account with a parent/guardian's permission before choosing this option.

If you find something that might look like a scam, tell an adult immediately. They can walk you through steps to report them to the proper authorities and shut them down so that they can't scam other people too.

Heading to the Bank

Do you remember going to the bank for the first time? Walking up to the teller and feeling like a grown-up was such a great feeling. The bank is where the money you earn will be kept.

There are machines that you can put your money into that directly transfers the amount inserted to your bank account. This is called an automatic teller machine (ATM), an electronic device that allows you to make transactions such as withdrawing money, depositing money, and checking your balance (Kagan, 2019). The ATM is convenient if the bank is not open for tellers. It is smart to use the personal teller as often as you can, especially for deposits, just to be more safe and accurate with your funds, but if they are not available, an ATM is a quick and easy way to transfer your money from your hands to the bank and vice versa.

Another important note is that if you use an ATM from a different bank, not your own, you will be charged a fee from your bank and from the bank you withdrew from. These bank charges can really add up, and if you just go to your bank's ATM, you will save yourself unnecessary fees. However these are not the only fees you have to worry about.

Banks will charge you a monthly fee for transactions, including eTransfers and bill payments. They will also charge you for these:

- Bouncing a check.
- Non-sufficient funds (NSF), meaning not having the funds in your bank and an automatic payment comes out.
- eTransfers, depending on your monthly plan.
- Going into overdraft, depending on your bank. Overdraft means taking out more money than you have in your account.
- Going over your allotted transactions (depending on

your account, you can get an idea of how many transactions you use. Unlimited transactions are available for a fee).

Overdraft protection is something you can apply for through your bank, if the bank decides you have good enough credit and have a long standing history with them. This means that you can protect your account by making it impossible for you to take out more money than is in your account. This keeps you from having a negative balance in your account and from getting fined for overdrafting.

It is important to keep your bank information private, especially your PIN number. Never share your personal information with anyone. If you lose your debit card, make sure you call the bank right away and let them know. They will help you get a new card and make sure your account was not used without your knowledge or permission. Some banks even have Smartphone apps that can let you lock your cards, making it impossible for anyone to use it until everything is fixed.

There's something a bank can offer called a certificate of deposit. This is an amount of money you give the bank, and it stays with the bank for a certain amount of time. You do not have to worry about losing the amount you invested because it is kept safe from inflation by the bank. Your return on investment and interest rates can be much higher with this kind of product. There are certain conditions to this as well, depending on your bank.

Okay, that was a lot to take in all at once. Let's talk about one of those big concepts. So ... what is inflation?

Inflation is the constant rise in the price of goods and services. Demand for goods pulls inflation, and cost of goods pushes it. When inflation is higher than what people are making, people stop buying things because goods and services are more expensive throughout the economy. It can be harmful for consumers and investors but can be beneficial to borrowers and lenders.

We talked about certificates of deposit, but those are not the only products a bank can offer. Check these out (Get it? Because we're talking about checks?):

eChecks: Instead of processing paper checks, these are processed digitally.

Electronic Funds Transfer: You can move your money from one account to another digitally.

Telebanking: From the convenience of your phone, you can check your balance, transfer funds, pay bills, and speak to a representative from the bank if you need any other assistance.

Mobile Banking: You can check all of the same things from telebanking, but it is from your Smartphone. Many of the major banks have their own app as well.

Internet Banking: All of the above can be done from the convenience of your laptop or computer.

Bet you didn't know that there were different kinds of savings accounts! Let me introduce to you the TFSA. What is a tax free savings account (TFSA), you might ask?

A TFSA is an account you can access with the money you save up, and it will be tax free up to a certain amount. You can collect interest on your total deposits, and once you decide to withdraw–depending on where you live–there is a maximum amount that you will not be charged tax on. A TFSA can also hold different investment types, such as mutual funds, bonds, and securities, which is a tradable financial asset.

Let's switch gears a little bit. We've talked about fees and charges and whatnot, but are there options out there that aren't charged with fees? Believe it or not, yes! We call it a guaranteed investment certificate, or GIC. The nice thing about a GIC is there are no charges or fees to purchase one. You will notice a better pay out if you can hold on to your GIC for a longer term, but you are easily able to cancel or close it.

There are three different types of GICs to choose from:

1. **Fixed Rate GIC:** This is the most popular type of GIC, and it can be a term of anywhere from three to

10 months. The great thing about a GIC is you are offered a guarantee back on your investment. You will earn interest on your principle, which is the original amount you put in, and won't lose any of that original principle if something were to happen.

2. **Variable Rate GIC:** Rates may change over time compared to a fixed rate GIC. You can benefit from good rates, but if they drop, you can also be affected negatively.

3. **Market/Equity-Linked GIC:** Your return on investment is based on how well the stock market is doing. (We will talk about stocks and bonds in chapter three.) If the market is performing well, your investment will grow, and if the market isn't performing well, your investment won't grow.

A big concept everyone needs to know about before heading out into the adult world is credit. There is something called a credit score that determines how good or bad your credit is. Or it could be non-existent, like yours probably is today. Don't worry though! You have lots of opportunities to build your credit. In the future when you want to get a loan from the bank, let's say to purchase a car, based on how good your credit is, you may or may not be approved for the loan.

So how do we avoid not getting that car with the disco ball, spinning seats, robot chef, and every song already uploaded into the radio? First, you need ways to build your credit:

1. **Pay your bills on time:** This includes cell phone bills, utility bills, or your cable bill.

2. **Get yourself a credit card:** Be careful with your credit card and start off with a very low credit limit. Choose a card that doesn't have an annual fee attached to it. This card should be used to build your credit, and when you use it to make a purchase, make sure you have that money in the bank to pay off the balance before interest accumulates (we will get into interest in the next chapter).

3. **Keep money in your savings:** Keeping a hefty amount of money in your savings account always looks good on your credit and shows you have a good ability to save.

When you apply for credit cards, car loans, or bank loans, the institution will collect your information to check on your credit score. Every time your credit score is looked at, you could be affected. It may even lower your score.

If you don't have a good credit score or even a credit history, most places won't grant you a loan. They may grant it if you can find yourself a co-signer. Be careful if you ever decide to co-sign something for someone else. If they end up not being able to make their payment, you are held responsible, and it could bring your credit score down if you cannot pay it.

Debt and bankruptcy: two of the scariest words in the money world. The best way to face something scary is to understand it. Let's talk about these two big, bad concepts and find out how we can protect ourselves against them.

Debt is the amount of money you owe someone. Debts can include personal injury debts, money you lent someone, and debts to the government. Also, when you get behind on your bills, such as credit cards, there are collection agencies that will call you daily. When you gather too much debt, you can go into something called bankruptcy.

Bankruptcy is legal and binding once you decide to file for it. It will stop collections from calling, and you can make an agreement on how much you will be able to afford monthly. Bankruptcy will stay on your record for seven to ten years (Tuovila, 2020). If you can use it as a last resort, that would be best since it does affect your credit score. You may have other options if you are able to come to some payment plan with your creditors. Your credit will be damaged, but you can always work on getting it back up to good standards.

Let's talk about ways we can protect ourselves against debt and bankruptcy. It is a really good idea to budget all the time. Keep track of what you are spending, and keep track of what you are saving. Do not spend above what you can handle. There are apps you can download on your phone to keep track of your spending and assist you with budgeting. Write down all of your bills and what you need to pay for, like groceries or gas for your car, and subtract it from what you earn monthly. You can even have automatic withdrawals from your bank. They can take out a certain amount that you wish for every week or every payday. That way it is doing the work for you if you forget, and as long as you don't touch it, you'll have a good savings for yourself.

It's easy to stay on top of your budget. Make sure you are constantly keeping track of what is coming in (income) and what is going out (bills and spending). Make a list of what you earn, and make a list of what your bills are that you absolutely have to have paid each month. What is left over is spending money. It is very important to try and take at least 20% of that for savings, and it is handy to have something put away in case of an emergency or just an unexpected cost.

There are lots of things you can do to save money in the smallest of ways. For example, if you buy milk or orange juice everyday from a convenience store or at school, you could be spending two to four dollars or more. Multiply that by five days a week, which is an average work week, and it could come out to $20 you could have been saving. That is an unnecessary cost you could easily avoid by drinking milk from home or bringing a cup of orange juice with you.

Here are some more budget tips to avoid debt and bankruptcy:

- Paying for cable can be expensive these days. You can pay up to $100 or more. There are streaming services out there, like Netflix, that start at only $9.99.

- Grocery shopping can be tricky. Make sure you try to look for special items on sale or that have coupons. If a certain staple for dinner is on sale, such as ground beef or chicken, then you can work around that staple for dinner.

- Meal planning is also key. When you set up your meals throughout the week early, you don't have to worry about spending extra money for food.

- Using cash for entertainment items can help you keep better track of your spending.

- Keep your receipts so you know what you are spending, or make sure to go over your monthly bank statements.

- Set up an automatic deposit on your savings account. Start out small, and if you can increase it later on, do so.

We can share our money with people who have less. When you get older, it is nice to have a charity you like to donate to. It is tax deductible, and it is nice to help those less fortunate. You can also feel more safe donating to a reputable charity. Unfortunately, there are a lot of scams out there, so be sure to do your research first.

We mentioned taxes briefly, but let's discuss them in more detail.

Every year, we are told to do our taxes. Taxes are an amount of money that we must pay the government according to how much we made the previous year. This money goes towards schools, building roads, and keeping our community safe and clean.

As soon as you are born, your parents can decide when you get a social insurance number or a social security card. You will need this to do lots of things in the future, like filing taxes. You will need it when you start working and want to collect your paycheck. When you work for a company, they will deduct a certain amount of taxes. At the end of the year, depending on how much taxes you paid and how much you earned, you will either owe the government money, or they will owe you money.

Taxes, fees, creditcards, deductibles, robot chefs… This is a lot to handle. Don't worry though. You still have plenty of time to learn and understand these concepts. And get a robot chef.

Once you understand the ideas from this chapter, go ahead and read the next one! It's time to get interest-ed in interests! (Get it? Because we're talking about interests?)

Chapter 2: Are You Interested in Interest?

Interest can be put into two categories: the kind that you give and the kind that you get. Interest can be good, like when you build interest on your savings account. Interest can also be bad, like when you owe money on your credit card. Here are just a few ways that interest will show up in your life.

When you borrow: Repay what you borrow, as well as the interest

When you save: The bank will pay you interest for keeping your money in the bank, which allows them to lend to other bank members.

When lending: You set a rate of interest and make profit off the money that you lent.

Wait, wait, wait. So the bank can just give us money for putting our money in their bank?! And there are options that can get you even more money?!

These magical, money-making accounts are called high interest savings accounts. High interest savings accounts can be beneficial because of the higher amount of interest you can make for each dollar saved.

Not-That-Simple Interest

What is simple interest?

Simple interest is just the interest that is built up overtime based *only* on the amount of money you originally put in.

What?

Okay, let's break it down with an equation.

To calculate simple interest, multiply the initial amount of money with the interest rate and then the time. Say I put $1 in the bank with a 10% interest. Because interest rates are decimal points, we will need to convert 10% to a decimal. Simply take the decimal and move it to the left twice! Once we multiple those two together, we'll get a number that is 10% of our original deposit. Multiply it by time–we'll pretend the interest is paid once a month–and we get our amount!

1 (our $1 dollar) x .10 (10% interest) x 12 (we want to see how much money we make in a year) = 1.2

In a year, we will make $1.20 just by keeping out money in the bank! We will end up with $2.20!

Interest is important to understand because there is good and bad interest. Every time you decide to take out a loan, you need to be aware of your interest rates. That could very much affect your ability to pay it back. If the interest is very high, then you will have a hard time paying back the amount you originally borrowed.

However, simple interest isn't the only kind of interest there is. There's also compound interest. This is interest that you earn on top of interest. It is a good thing if you have a savings account that is earning interest on top of interest because your money will definitely grow faster. Compound interest can be harder on us if it is money that we owe though. If you have compound interest on a loan, it will be very hard to even make a dent in paying the original amount.

The best compound interest investments:

1. Certificates of deposits
2. High interest savings accounts
3. Rental properties
4. Bonds (see chapter three)
5. Stocks (see chapter three)

6. Treasury securities: When the government needs money to pay debts, or has a plan for something new, you can get treasury bills, and if you wait until it matures, you will profit from it.

Then there are the other interests we don't want hanging around. The interest on our credit cards. When you apply for a credit card, and you are approved, you can start making purchases like we mentioned earlier to help build your credit. You have to be careful not to spend beyond your means or make a large purchase, knowing you don't have the money to pay it off. The best way to be smart with your credit card, while achieving some credit history, is to make a few purchases here and there and keep the balance paid off. The interest accumulated from holding a credit card balance can be 20% or higher, so be careful how much you spend!

Just as it is smart to keep credit card balance low or zero, it is important to be aware of the loans we decide to take out. If they are borrowed from a trustworthy company, and if the financing and interest rates are not too high, we can feel more confident in where our money is going.

Let's Talk About Equity

Equity is the value of your assets after subtracting what you still owe on it.

There are two types of equity:

1. **Book Value:** There is an equation to figure out market equity: assets minus liabilities. Assets are what you own, and liability is what you owe.

2. **Market Value:** Equity is described as market value. That would include what you have invested in the stock market, so the market value will be constantly changing due to the shareholders, investors, etc.

There is something you may have heard of called a mortgage. This is something you can get when you want to purchase a home. Mortgages have simple interest, but because you are paying the interest up front, it takes longer to pay the principle, which is the amount you originally borrowed. That would be the same for a car. Most car companies will base the interest rate off how good your credit is. If you have a very high interest rate, it will be much harder to pay down the principle.

Equity can go up and down, but there are specific things that go up and down. What goes up in value?

Things like your home will improve their value over time. You can buy a home that needs work, and if you have the time and skills, you can fix it up with several renovations, and the market value of your home will increase. Another reason houses go up so much in value is if there are not enough houses being built to keep up with the demand.

What goes down in value?

Items like cars go down in value, or depreciate. According to current rates, a car can depreciate by more than 20% after just one year. The car will continue to depreciate at a rate of about 10% per year for the next four years. By the end of five years of ownership, you're looking at the possibility of your vehicle being worth about 40% of the price you originally paid for it (Car Depreciation: Why Do New Cars Lose Value So Quickly?, n.d.-b).

This is because the parts of the car do not last long from everyday wear and tear. The demand for cars is not as high as housing. There are constantly new models coming out each year, and that affects the value of your car. The resale value is just so low. Once your car leaves the lot, sadly it is considered 'used'.

Your best bet to save money is not to purchase a vehicle brand new. As much as it may seem like the best choice, you are saving so much more in the long run if you go with a used car. If you can save up for the total amount of the vehicle, or get an older model and get a bank loan with potentially lower interest rates, you are much better off. Just make sure you do research to make sure the car is in good working shape. Hire a mechanic to take a look and make sure nothing will go wrong with it too soon. In the end, it will be more worth it to pay for a mechanic one time to make sure you are in a safe vehicle.

Real Estate

Buying a home will be one of the most important decisions you make in your lifetime. It is a great milestone that many people try to achieve. Paying off your mortgage sooner than later is always what people strive for. It involves a lot of research, not only on the pricing and market, but also the community and neighbors.

More tips on finding your forever home:

- Consider the location and if there are amenities nearby, such as grocery stores or other shopping malls.

- Make sure you're not living in a neighborhood surrounded by renters.

- Consider the neighborhood and if it is low in crime.

- Consider the location and if you want to be close to other family members or not.

- Your budget should come into play because some areas have a higher cost of living than others.

- The climate may be important to you, so if you don't like hot or cold weather, keep that in mind.

- If you have pets, consider getting a home with a nice backyard.

- Living near good schools may be something you eventually might consider as well.

- If you don't own a vehicle, research the transit routes and if they are convenient in your area.

There are a lot of words used in real estate that you should become familiar with that will help you better understand the process.

- **Appraisal:** This determines the value of your home at the time of purchase and what your mortgage will look like after.

- **Buyer's agent:** This agent helps the buyer during the selling process.

- **Buyer's market:** This is where supply is higher than the demand, so the buyer's have an advantage over the sellers.

- **Closing:** The sale of the property is final.

- **Home warranty:** In case of unexpected costs for plumbing or anything else, this will be covered for rental owners.

- **Inspection:** This is important to do before you purchase a property to make sure everything is up to good standards.

- **Pre-approval letter:** The lender will write a letter for the buyer to let them know that they are able to borrow money.

- **Real estate market analysis:** This is research done to know if a certain market is profitable.

- **Realtor:** This person helps you purchase or sell a property, and they are very knowledgeable in the field of real estate.

- **Refinancing:** You can recieve a lower interest rate by trading an old home loan for a new one.

- **Sellers market:** This is where there is less demand or a shortage for property, so sellers have the advantage over the buyers.

- **Closing costs:** This is costs such as taxes and other processing fees and costs that you have to pay when you close on a house.

- **Comparative market analysis:** This is to compare with other houses around to determine the market value

- **Foreclosure:** The bank takes your home when you don't pay your mortgage

It is important to know there will always be a supply and demand depending on certain demographics, the economy, or housing market crashes. Be sure to do plenty of research when you start looking for a home, and always watch the trends in prices and the different markets. And remember, when you get to that process, have fun with it!

Chapter 3: The Good, the Bad, and the Ugly Investments

Investing your money can be very beneficial, but it can also be tricky. It involves being committed to putting your money into something in hopes for a great financial return. Investing is a bit different in that you are saving your money, but when you invest for a long period of time, you will reap more of the rewards.

Investments are a good way to make money if you are committed. Of course, with any investment, there is a risk, so be aware of that. Take the right risks and be smart, especially until you are out of the beginners stage. Bottom line is it takes a lot of patience and plenty of research to make good money with investments.

Going back to real estate, this can be a good investment choice if you are aware of some of the types. Investing in multiple real estate properties is a great way to make a hefty income. You can buy multiple properties and earn the money off renting them to other people, or you can fix them up like mentioned earlier, making quite a profit.

There are some ways you can use real estate investments in different ways to make a hefty profit.

1. **Rental properties:** This is a good way to make money by buying a home, making sure it is appealing to possible renters, and collecting rent from them. You can also rent out long term or short term. However, you are responsible for all of the things that go wrong around the house and keeping up the repairs.

2. **Airbnb:** If you are willing to start an Airbnb, that is for more of a short-term tenant to rent out.

3. **Buy and hold:** This is when you purchase a home and hold on to it until the market goes up, and then you can sell it at a higher price and make a nice profit. Of course, this is more long term.

4. **Fix and flip:** This is a popular way to earn money, but it does take a lot of work since you are purchasing the property and doing all the work to fix it up. It will also require a team of professionals to help you with things like plumbing, electric, etc.

5. **Real estate investment trust (REIT):** This requires much less work than the other real estate investments because you are investing in a property almost like you would a stock or a share, so you just have to wait on your investment to flourish.

If you are like some, you have your reasons for not wanting to own a property. Maybe you don't have enough saved for a deposit on a home. Some people prefer to rent so they don't have to take care of all the extra costs and labor to upkeep a home. For whatever reason you chose, there are some things you should know when it comes to renting, whether that be a home, a suit, a blow up bouncy house, or a robot chef.

- Make sure you have a proper lease, in writing, signed by all parties with all the terms and requirements.
- Find out the date rent is due, and make sure you understand the penalties that come along with late payments.
- If you have a pet, make sure you understand the policies on that and if there is an extra charge. Normally they will charge you half of the rent.
- Make sure you find out if you are responsible for the lawn or snow removal.
- You will have a deposit to give for any damages that

may occur while you reside there, so make sure you understand what that means. Some things, like putting up pictures and putting holes in the wall, can be considered 'normal wear and tear' depending on the length of the lease agreement.

- Make sure you understand the rules of noise laid out in your lease agreement.

- Any other terms there may be, for example, what is and is not allowed on the deck if you have one.

Stocks and Bonds
What are stocks?

Stocks are a type of investment where you can choose the company you see on the market to invest in. In other words, you can buy a small piece of the company. Stocks are tricky because they can go up, and the next day, they could plummet. You are worse off if you don't invest in multiple types of companies–this is called diversifying–as well. Before getting started, find out what kind of fees you may have with your investments. It is easy to access through an online investment platform.

Let's talk more about diversification. Diversification is when you spread your investments throughout different types of companies. The risk of losing a bigger chunk of money is less. It's like the old saying goes, "Don't put all your eggs in one basket." If one of your investments is not doing as well, you won't end up losing everything because maybe another company is doing better.

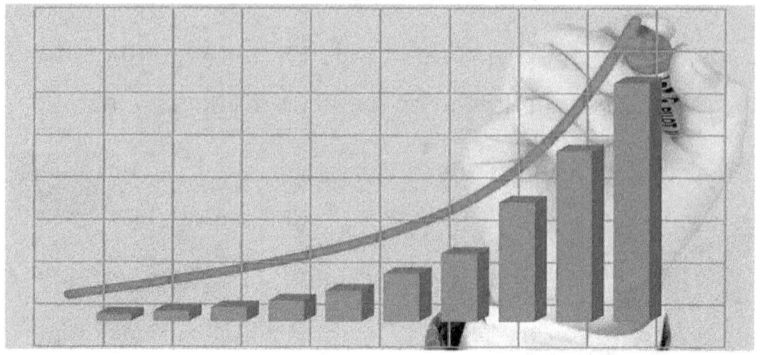

What are bonds?

Bonds are a loan, and the borrower has to pay it back at a certain time. There are government bonds and corporate bonds. They are less risky than stocks. You are lending your money to a company or organization, so you are the person loaning out money. When the bond matures, the lender pays back the amount.

There is something in the bond world called a return on investment (ROE). This measures what you get back, compared to what you put in. You may invest some money in your business or just invest much of your own time. This is not the same thing as profit, which is your expenses subtract your income. ROE can be helpful with your business to figure out if what you are doing for the business is helpful or just a waste of time. To calculate your ROE, which you should be doing frequently in your business, you divide your net benefits by your total cost.

Now let's talk about something called liquidity. Liquidity refers to the ability to convert capital (wealth of assets you have) to cash without affecting its market price.

Once you graduate high school, continuing your education is crucial in the future of the career world. The sooner you can start to put away some money, the better. You can open up what is called a RESP. This stands for registered education savings plan. This is a good way to keep money in a separate account that is harder to get at and be tempted to spend. The bonus with an RESP is the government will help you by contributing as well.

An RRSP is a registered retirement savings plan, which is also important to know about for your future. It has been around for over 60 years! You can set one up and have some peace of mind knowing you have something saved up for after you retire from working. Most people retire around the age of 60-65. Certain jobs will put funds toward your retirement, but if your employer does not offer anything like that, it is important to set something up for yourself. The great thing about an RRSP is the government will allow you to add a certain amount, and that amount is deducted from your earning income. For example, if you make $60,000 a year and contribute $8,200, when it's time to file for your taxes, the government will act as if you only made $51,800 (Goldman, 2021).

Remember: No matter what, investments will always come with a risk. High/low risk/reward is a measure of how much risk you are taking in your investments and what kind of return or reward you will be getting. The ratio would be profit divided by loss. It is important to see how much risk you take for each trade.

There are a few investments out there that are not so beneficial. Take a look at these investments to stay away from!

1. **Timeshare:** This is when you purchase a property with a group of people, but you must share the property throughout the year. The amount you invest in will not be worth it.
2. **Restaurants:** There is a lot of work involved in keeping a restaurant open and thriving. You also have to hire proper staff, from cooks to wait staff, not to mention the fierce competition.
3. **Penny Stocks:** These are stocks that are cheap, and people think they can find the next big thing at a very

low cost, but they are not properly regulated and are hard to trade.

4. Do not invest in anything you are not familiar with. Do lots of research on the background and history of the company, etc.

Cryptocurrency

Cryptocurrency is talked about all over the place these days. It is a digital form of payment used to purchase goods or services online. There are more than 10,000 types of cryptocurrencies. Companies use them like tokens, and they can be traded for the goods or services of certain companies.

Cryptocurrency uses a technology called blockchain which is helpful with keeping transactions online secure, as well as managing and keeping track of transactions. Everyone wants to snatch up some crypto before it is much more valuable. Most people like the fact that the bank is less involved with their funds.

Now the question is, are they a good investment? Just like real currencies, cryptocurrencies generate no cash flow, so for you to gain any profit, someone else has to pay more for the currency than you paid. Many people consider the idea unstable.

To purchase cryptocurrency, you need what is called an online wallet. You can then transfer real money to buy your cryptocurrency. Are they legal? Yes and no. They are considered legal, but countries have banned them.

Always remember 'buyer beware' because this is a good opportunity for those scammers to try and get you. Just remember to be smart and protect yourself.

The most popular type of cryptocurrency is Bitcoin.

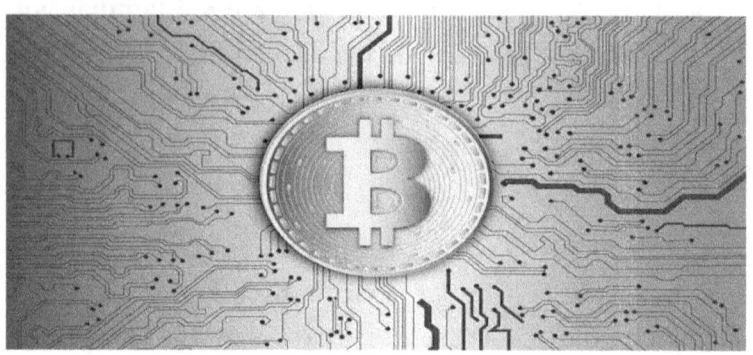

Why is bitcoin so popular? The value of bitcoin, to everyone's surprise, skyrocketed a couple of times in the past, and is continuing to soar. Now a lot of other types of cryptocurrencies are starting to rise in value, and everyone wants a piece of the pie. Bitcoin was created in 2018 by Satoshi Nakamoto, an anonymous person or group of people, and it is still just as popular as it was when it first began.

There is definitely future potential in this type of currency. It is so popular because of the user-friendly perks. It provides people with a certain level of anonymity while having lower general fees, and it is self-sustainable.

Meet Jaydyn Carr

Jaydyn Carr is a ten-year-old boy from San Antonio that made some good investments and cashed in on his smart choices with his money. Back in 2019, Jaydyn was given ten GameStop shares, each at $6.19, from his mother. GameStop is a video game company, and his mother bought the shares because of her son's love for the games. His $60 stake in the company quickly grew to $3,200! After Jaydyn's mother taught him all about the stock market, he made the good decision to sell his stock and keep his money. There was always a chance he could lose it all. Jaydyn decided to keep $1,000 of his money to further invest with his mother and put the rest in a savings account.

This story goes to show that you never know what can happen to your money, and being smart about putting it away will make you appreciate the value of a dollar and how to manage money. Besides, how cool is it to own a bit of your favorite company?

CONCLUSION

So you think you know everything about money? Well, you have learned a lot about it, and you know so much more than you did yesterday, but there is still a lot out there to learn. It's not just what you know, it's about what you do with your newfound knowledge and the decisions you make for yourself. It may seem like a lot to take in, so just take your time with what you want to learn, and when you want to achieve something for the future, know that you can do it. You are the one who is going to make the future the brightest you want it to be.

Saving is Super

Now that you know a lot of the basics of money and much more, the good and the bad, start saving for the future, but don't be afraid to have fun once in a while. You work hard for your money, and you deserve a splurge every once in a while too.

Planning your personal finances is a very important activity that you should always keep on top of. It helps you to understand where your money is going on a regular basis.

It is never too early to begin personal finance. You should do it as soon as you start to earn your allowance. Talk to a parent or guardian, and make a plan together. You can always come up with some great ideas and brainstorm where your money should go and how you can earn it while still keeping focus on your school and having fun of course!

Just remember: Be smart with your money, and never stop learning about ways to save and spend wisely. If you ever need tips to help you get started in the world of money, this book is here for you. So go out there, make some money, give back to the community, get that robot chef, and be confident in the world of finances!

REFERENCES

7 Ways to Save Money on a Tight Budget. (2014). The Balance. https://www.thebalance.com/how-to-save-when-money-is-tight-2386118

Anderson, H. (2018, September 26). *What is compound interest, and is it good or bad?* CUInsight. https://www.cuinsight.com/what-is-compound-interest-and-is-it-good-or-bad.html#:~:text=If%20you%20have%20a%20savings%20or%20investment%20account%2C

andreas160578. (2017 March 9). *Lawn mower lawn mowing rush mow.* [Image]. https://pixabay.com/photos/lawn-mower-lawn-mowing-rush-mow-2127637/

anncapictures. (2017 November 7). *Toy cash register play money.* [Image]. https://pixabay.com/photos/toy-cash-register-play-money-2922214/

Bennett, P. (2021, June 11). *Avoid these 10 of the worst investments ever.* MyBankTracker. https://www.mybanktracker.com/news/avoid-worst-investments-ever

Bru-nO. (2015 October 29). *Thumb hand human gesture.* [Image]. https://pixabay.com/photos/thumb-hand-human-gesture-1006395/

BYJUS. (2021). *What is equity? Meaning, definition, market value, examples.* BYJUS. https://byjus.com/commerce/what-is-equity/

Car depreciation: Why do new cars lose value so quickly? (n.d.). Bryant Motors. https://www.bryantmotors.com/car-buying-guide/car-depreciation-guide.html

Compare & apply loans & credit cards in India. (2020, August 19). Paisabazaar.com. https://www.paisabazaar.com/mutual-funds/certificate-of-deposit/

Elmin Media. (2021, January 25). *Why Bitcoin is the most popular cryptocurrency?* EconoTimes. https://econotimes.com/Why-Bitcoin-Is-The-Most-Popular-Cryptocurrency-1600819#:~:text=The%20second%20reason%20as%20to%20why%20Bitcoin%20is

flyerwerk. (2016 October 19). *EC Cash paymentsatm money cashless.* [Image]. https://pixabay.com/photos/ec-cash-paymentsatm-money-cashless-1750490/

Francis, A. (2010, August 21). *Different products and services offered by banks.* MBA Knowledge Base. https://www.mbaknol.com/business-finance/different-products-offered-by-banks/

geralt. (2018 May 15). *Save piggy bank money coins.* [Image].

https://pixabay.com/photos/save-piggy-bank-money-coins-3402476/

geralt. (2017 June 15). *Learn mathematics child girl.* https://pixabay.com/photos/learn-mathematics-child-girl-2405206/

Goldman, A. (2021a). *Investing 101: Investing basics for beginners.* Wealthsimple. https://www.wealthsimple.com/en-ca/learn/investing-basics#types_of_investments

Goldman, A. (2021b, April 21). *What is an RRSP? Retire the smart way.* Wealthsimple. https://www.wealthsimple.com/en-ca/learn/what-is-rrsp#benefits_of_the_registered_retirement_savings_plan

Hamed, E. (2018, April 3). *7 Things to know before renting out a house as an investment property.* Investment Property Tips | Mashvisor Real Estate Blog. https://www.mashvisor.com/blog/things-to-know-before-renting-out-a-house

Horizon Trust Team. (2019, August 1). *What are the best compound interest investments? Top 7 picks.* Horizon Trust. https://www.horizontrust.com/what-are-the-best-compound-interest-investments-top-7-picks/#:~:text=%20Top%207%20Picks%20%201%20CDs.%2020Considered

International Association of Better Business Bureaus, Inc. (2021). *BBB tips: 10 Steps to avoid scams.* Better Business Bureaus, Inc. https://www.bbb.org/article/scams/8767-bbb-tips-10-steps-to-avoid-scams

Janet Berry-Johnson. (2018, September 25). *How to build credit fast.* Self. https://www.self.inc/blog/how-to-build-credit

jarmoluk. (2014 February 1). *Money card business credit card.* [Image]. https://pixabay.com/photos/money-card-business-credit-card-256319/

jarmoluk. (2014 August 27). *Document agreement documents sign.* [Image]. https://pixabay.com/photos/document-agreement-documents-sign-428334/

jarmoluk. (2017 November 8). *ATM money cash payment finance.* [Image]. https://pixabay.com/photos/atm-money-cash-payment-finance-2923515/

jaydeep_. (2018 January 20). *Bitcoin currency technology money.* [Image]. https://pixabay.com/illustrations/bitcoin-currency-technology-money-3089728/

Kagan, J. (2019a). *Automated teller machine - ATM.* Investopedia. https://www.investopedia.com/terms/a/atm.asp

Kagan, J. (2019b). *Compound interest definition.* Investopedia. https://www.investopedia.com/terms/c/compoundinterest.asp

Larisa-K. (2013 July 19). *House countryside architecture.* [Image]. https://pixabay.com/illustrations/house-countryside-architecture-163526/

Martucci, B. (2021). *11 Tips to find the best neighborhood to live in.* Money Crashers. https://www.moneycrashers.com/tips-find-best-neighborhood-live-in/

MaryByrne. (2017 February 22). *Green money finance cash currency*. [Image]. https://pixabay.com/vectors/green-money-finance-cash-currency-2084561/

MBURUGU, C. (2020, January 23). *Everything you need to know about real estate*. Investment Property Tips | Mashvisor Real Estate Blog. https://www.mashvisor.com/blog/everything-you-need-to-know-about-real-estate/#:~:text=%20Everything%20You%20Need%20to%20Know%20About%20Real

Mediamodifier. (2017 March 13). *eCommerce selling online*. [Image]. https://pixabay.com/photos/ecommerce-selling-online-2140604/

mohamed_hassan. (2020 August 31). *Money cash tree watering hand*. [Image]. https://pixabay.com/vectors/money-cash-tree-watering-hand-5530537/

Neecey. (2021a, July 15). *7 Fascinating facts from the history of money ... All Women's Talk*. https://money.allwomenstalk.com/fascinating-facts-from-the-history-of-money/#7

Neecey. (2021b, July 15). *7 Fascinating facts from the history of money ... All Women's Talk*. https://money.allwomenstalk.com/fascinating-facts-from-the-history-of-money/#7

Page, S. (2021, January 30). *"Is this really happening right now?": A 10-year-old cashes in his GameStop shares*. Washington Post. https://www.washingtonpost.com/lifestyle/2021/01/30/gamest

op-kwanzaa-kid-stock/

Pritchard, J. (2021, June 23). *How to calculate simple interest.* The Balance. https://www.thebalance.com/simple-interest-overview-and-calculations-315578

QuinceCreative. (2017 October 26). *Piggy bank money finance banking.* [Image]. https://pixabay.com/illustrations/piggy-bank-money-finance-banking-2889042/

stevepb. (2015 August 10). *Shopping spending till slip.* [Image]. https://pixabay.com/photos/shopping-spending-till-slip-879498/

stevepb. (2015 October 30). *Coins calculator budget.* [Image]. https://pixabay.com/photos/coins-calculator-budget-1015125/

Tax-free savings account (TFSA). (2020, July 22). Investopedia. https://www.investopedia.com/terms/t/tax-free-savings-account-tfsa.asp#:~:text=Key%20Takeaways%201%20Tax-free%20savings%20accounts%20%28TFSAs%29%20are

Techboomers. (2018). *What is PayPal? How does it work? - Free tutorial on TechBoomers.* TechBoomers.com. https://techboomers.com/t/what-is-paypal#:~:text=So%20what%20exactly%20is%20PayPal%3F%20PayPal%20is%20a

Tuovila, A. (2020, May 15). *Bankruptcy definition.* Investopedia. https://www.investopedia.com/terms/b/bankruptcy.asp

Tumisu. (2015 January 27). *Profits revenue business income.* [Image]. https://pixabay.com/illustrations/profits-revenue-business-income-1953616/

Tumisu. (2020 June 15). *Investment growth watering can.* [Image]. https://pixabay.com/photos/investment-growth-watering-can-5299600/

What is a GIC - Types, features and restrictions. (n.d.). Ratehub.ca. Retrieved July 13, 2021, from https://www.ratehub.ca/gics/what-is-a-gic

What is inflation? (2021, July 10). The Balance. https://www.thebalance.com/what-is-inflation-357610

What is return on investment (ROI)? (2019). The Balance Small Business. https://www.thebalancesmb.com/roi-return-on-investment-1794432

www.ingramcontent.com/pod-product-compliance
Lightning Source LLC
Chambersburg PA
CBHW070855220526
45466CB00005B/2003